ANCIENT INDIAN COMMERCE

COMMERCIAL RELATIONS OF INDIA IN THE MIDDLE EAST

Republished By

Charlies Publication, India

[f1]The imperial Romans flashed their sword both in the East and the West with different results. In the East " they conquered the world only to give it to " [f2](........) in the West however " they either Romanised the races who were at first their subjects [f3](. . . . . .) masters, or left those races to be the willing agents of their own Romanisation." [f4] As a result of this Romanisation the West is proud of her heritage from the Romans. How this rich heritage was accumulated none has taken pains to inquire into.

Justly may we look to the Romans for their military Organisation, the elaboration of law and the wonderful discipline of hordes levied before war and discharged after victory. Hemmed in from all sides—the Etruscans pressing in from the north, the Lygurians from the West, the Sabians from the East and the Greeks from the South, the Latins' summoned the energy by despair. Excepting perhaps the women and youngsters of both sexes the entire population was one huge militia ever ready to rally round the red flag at the call of a trumpet. But Rome gathered in energy too voluminous for the space she had and illustrated the principle that concentration causes explosion and expansion. Goaded by the greed of territory or pressed on by the mania of foreign persecution she started first by consuming the entire Italian peninsula. But imperialism conscious or unconscious knows no stop. Rome by sheer prowess of her arms went on in her career of conquest and made war her only noble profession. She knew not that war like competition destroys itself. In one great sweep, she brought an immense territory under her control but left the circle of her extensive imperium to shrink back towards the center when the propelling energy from within had, as it was sure to be, exhausted itself.

Beside their military exploits and inhuman gladiatorial feats, the Romans (owed)[f5] credit from the art of road-building and administration; these arts are quite natural and necessary concomitants of imperialism. (Beside these)*[f6] there (was)*[f7] little of the Roman contribution to civilization that cannot be summed up in the phrase *pax Romana.*

Underneath the canopy of Roman Imperialism there was a constant and" peaceful infiltration ", (of the East)*. Philosophy, astronomy, mathematics, medicine constitute her bequests. Scholarship incompatible with the practical genius of the Romans, was the trade of the Orientals. The Roman Court was begemmed by the stars from the East. Egypt lays claim to Ptolemy and Plotinus: Porphyry and Iamblichus are the sons of Syria while Dioscorides and Galen were Asiatics. 'Much of the Roman Civilization was made up by the doings of the Eastern slaves who even conducted the education of the Roman children in the public schools established under the empire. Romans were' the lovers of the powerful rather than of the beautiful: "Rome, in herself inartistic, enlaned art and artists for her own purpose. Her barbaric delight in vivid colouring, which for instance, was exhibited in the gold and scarlet decoration on the great column of Trojan, was stimulated by eastern commerce "[f8]. Even Roman architecture is the product of the oriental slaves. The entire strength of Rome was spent in conquest or if we choose, in the struggle for existence. But after enough of struggle she might have as well utilized the leisure which was hers and availed herself of the varied geniuses brought within her compass by her subject people. Unfortunately Rome never realized or it was too late (that she)* did that "peace hath her victories no less renowned than war " and (her)* militarism pure and simple is thrown in great relief when we notice the (.........)* fact that" although Rome raised a statue to Quiet, she (.........)[f9] out (........)* walls "[f10]. Though Rome had some industries, her productive capacity was miserably low; her consumption overran her production which necessitated continual drain of specie. The Latefundia destroyed her agriculture and (drove)* the farmers to beggary and made Rome entirely dependent for her food on Sicily and Egypt. Owing to the great concentration of landed property the land had ceased to be productive, and there was practically no Italian harvest. She received everything mostly from the East and nothing or little to give in return.

" It is in the orient, especially in these countries of old civilization that we must look for industry and riches for technical ability and artistic productions as well as for intelligence and science, even before Constantine made it [Rome] the center of political power ".[f11] Nay " all branches of learning were affected by the spirit of the orient "[f12] which " was her superior in extent and precision of its technical knowledge as well as in the inventive genius and ability of its workman " [f13]Descending from the productions of industrial arts to those of industry itself, one .might also trace the growing influence of the Orient: one might show how the action of the great manufacturing centers of the East gradually transformed the material civilization of Europe ; one might point out how the introduction in Gaul of Exotic patterns and processes changed the old native industry and gave (their)* products a perfection and a popularity hitherto unknown. "[f14]From time immemorial upto the Industrial Revolution, the East enjoyed (the)* pre-eminence of being the workshop of the world and it is significant to (note that)* she was busy in producing the wonderful and massive iron columns that attest to the mechanics and technique of the time when chipping a stone and making a hatchet was a superhuman task with the Western neolith.

Thus " the East gave (impe)[f15] tus to the West. "[f16] It is in the valley of the Nile, the Euphrates, the Yangtse Kang and the Indus that we first witness the misty dawn of civilization, the beginning of knowledge and progress. " To have caught the light from the East and reflected it with manifold luster on the West is the only work of Greece and Rome. "[f17]

Looked at from this angle the dragon of" Dark Ages " seems to be a fictitious creation of the historian. Were there any such Dark ages in Europe ? If so, when was there light ? History does not disclose it. Whatever light or civilization there was, was confined to the Eastern basin of the Mediterranean [being constantly fed by the Orient] barring which the entire continent of Europe was in barbarism till very late : the Curve of European Civilization (leaving aside the sources on which it drew) is constantly rising and what the historian calls Dark ages mark a point of civilization higher than the one reached by preceding centuries. The fiction of the ' Dark ages ' arose from the fallacy of the thinking of whole of Europe in terms of Rome, but nothing is more false than to think of the whole in terms of a part.

To be true to facts the question of the ' Dark Ages ' has to be raised (by the) historian of the Orient. It is he who has to answer why this great (fall) after a high crest, why this sudden darkness after the (dawn):

It is lamentable to see that the earliest and most promising civilizations ran into a blind alley and were arrested all of a sudden when progress was most expected of them. Some of these early civilizations died out leaving us their records on bricks and tablets. Others are lingering on in their way and are in the process of rejuvenation.

The civilization of India is one of the oldest but like all of them has come to a dead stop : but it has lived to revive and we may hope never to die again. The contact of the west has shaken the " fixity " and restored her old dynamic power.

Historians often wonder why civilization begins at one particular spot rather than at another. Is it because of the ability of the inhabitants ? Or is it because that providence wills them their civilization ? A short consideration will convince us that both these factors play the second fiddle. The first is played by environment. Given a bountiful environment and chances of conservation, isolation or security from foreign invasion, civilization is bound to sprout forth.

India's geographical position just fitted her to be the Early craddle of civilization. Nature has given her that isolation that has been the envy of many of tribal people who are ever in search of a secure abode to develop their capacity and make the most of nature's gifts. Severed from China and Tibet on the north by the Himalaya mountains, on the East from Burma and Assam by the Tenasserim and on the west from Afghanistan by the (Karakoram)[f18] (Hindukush)* Ranges the entire peninsula forms a world in miniature in itself—(formed)* by strong natural defenses— "

the mountains "[f19] forming " a wall on the North-West and the sea. . a moat on all other sides. "

This " inverted triangle " conserves the most varied and most abundant of natural resources. "Animal life is not only abundant in British India, but it is remarkably varied. The number of kinds of animals inhabiting India and its dependencies is very large, far surpassing, for instance, that of the species found in the whole of Europe, although the superficial area of Europe exceeds that of the Indian empire by about one-half "[f20]Equally is her rich diversity of flora and fauna and her climate that makes possible the existence of such variegated animal life. The richness of vegetable life is unbounded. All these factors have from time immemorial combined to bestow upon her the economic self-sufficiency which has been the privilege of a few nations on the face of this planet today.

Given the materials, man can hardly be expected to remain inactive for the economic motive is the strongest and the most dynamic of all. He tries at once to exploit the environment for his well-being and the early inhabitants of India were no exception to the rule. It would be a mistake if we take a modem average Indian as a prototype of his stalwart ancestor. He may resemble him perhaps in features but that's all. The semblance ends there. The India of antiquity within the span of time in which he held the undisputed possession of the country accomplished much more than could be expected of primitive. We have scanty records of his deeds but what little we have and as will be seen from the following narrative, speaks volumes.

Of the multifarious achievements of the ancient Indians, important as they are, we are not concerned. We have to center our attend on their economic activity alone.

At the outset it would be better to take note of the lampposts or the sources that will help us in our survey. On the nature side there is a lamentable paucity. The Hindoos are loquacious on everything except the economic activity of their life and the reason is not far to see. Education was monopolized by a class of people who were more or less " drones in the hive, gorging at a feast to which they [had] contributed nothing ". The Brahamin or the intellectual caste of India enjoyed " the conspicuous leisure " and " the- conspicuous consumption " vicariously ; consequently the economic activity of the ancient Hindoos found no exponents and no mention in the literature which is purely sacerdotal. This also explains why India did not produce any literature on the Science of Economic as such. Hence we are" compelled to depend entirely on foreign authorities and their scanty reference to India's commerce.

Before we launch on the subject of commerce we shall do better to take hasty survey of the Economic development of Ancient India. There is no authority on the subject that can take us back to the pre-Buddha times. The Buddha Jatakas— the birth-stories of Buddha—are the earliest source on the subject and contain literary references to the economic organisation of the Indian society which may be supposed to have existed from times very remote from the dates of these Jatakas ....

1. Agricultural Organisation:

Very early we find the ancient Hindoos living a village life : Each village consisted of from 30 to 1000 families. No isolated houses were to be found but they clustered together. Agriculture is known as the highest occupation and the Indian proverb puts the merchantman second to the farmer and the soldier occupies the last place in social gradation.

Land was cultivated by the farmer and his families and some times by hired labour. " The traditional feeling was apparently against land transfer ". Yet we see that land was rented out for cultivation. Independent landholder was regarded respectfully but work on the farm of a capitalist was greatly i disapproved. There is no evidence to definite say whether or not there was feudalism in village community.

There was a great deal of co-operation among villagers for building and repairing roads and tanks and municipal buildings :

" The sovereign claimed an annual *tilha* on raw produce. This was levied, and in kind amounted to 1/6, 1/8, 1/10 or 1/12." " Grain, pulse, and sugarcane were the chief products: vegetables, possibly also fruit and flowers were cultivated. Rice was reckoned as the staple article of food."

Agriculture was a common occupation for even we see the Brahmin figuring as a goatherd and both as a small and large landholder without losing his caste. The love of the ancient Hindoo and for that matter of the modem for agriculture transcends that of the ancient Greek and is just manifested in the worship of the cow.

The Hindoo devotion to the Cow has been an enigma to most of the foreigners and above all has been an efficient lore in the hands of those half-baked theological failures who go to India to conduct their missionary propaganda for blackmailing the Hindoo.

The origin of cow worship is as much economic as that Roman practice of not offering wine to the Gods from unpruned vines. The cow and for that matter all draft animals, is the soul of the farmers. The cow gives birth to oxen which are absolutely necessary to the cultivation of the farm. If we kill the cow for meat, we jeopardize our agricultural prosperity. With full foresight, the ancient Hindoos tabooed cow-flesh and thus prevented cow killing. But man hardly pays any attendon to dry rulings. It must have religious sanction; hence the grotesque mythology around the cow in old Hindoo religious literature.

II. Organisation of Labour, Industry and Commerce:

Be it said to the credit of the Hindoos that slavery paid a very little role in their economic life. Capture, judicial punishment, voluntary self-degradation and debt were the four principal causes by which individuals become slaves. But there is considerable evidence to show that kindly treatment was the rule and manumission was always possible. Besides few slaves there was a considerable amount of free-labour paid in money or food.

From among the industrial classes the following are mentioned :—

(a) The *vaddhaki* is a .genuine term and is an embodiment of a carpenter, ship-builder, cart-maker and an architect.

(b) The *Kammara* is a generic term for a metal craftsman producing " iron implement, from a ploughshare or an axe or for that matter, an iron house, down to a razor, or the finest of needles, capable of floating in water, or again, statues of gold or silver work."

(c) The *Pasanakottaka* is a generic term for a mason " not only quarrying and shaping stones. .. .. but as capable of hallowing a cavity in a crystal, a matter probably of requiring superior tools."

" A considerable degree of Organisation characterized all the trading industries. Certain trades were localised in special villages, either suburban and ancillary to the large cities, or themselves forming centres of traffic with surounding villages e. g. the woodwork and metal work industries and pottery........... within the cities trades appear to have been localized in special streets e. g. those of ivory workers and of dyers."

The trades were well regulated and were superintended by one or two headmen who were the chiefs or syndics of municipal and industrial Organisation of the cities.

There were numerous guilds (*Seniyo*) under the headship of a President *(Prarnukha)* or elder or older man *(Jethaka).*

Carpenters, smiths, leather workers, painters, and experts in various arts had their grids. Even the sea-men garland-makers and caravan traders.

There was a tendency towards hereditary occupation. But the caste system in all its hideous rigorousness was not present and even Brahmins were often occupied in low professions.

There was little riverine traffic : it was mostly conducted by the caravans. The industrial centres were connected by good roads which greatly facilitated traffic. The Ramayana refers to a road starting out from Ayodhya the capital of King Dasharatha, known presently as Oudh to Rajagriha the capital of Kekayas in the vicinity of the Himalaya mountains situated on the River Bias, the ancient Vipasa known to the Greeks as the Hypasis passed through Hasdnapur (Delhi) the capital of the Kurus. Alexander's information regarding the roads in ancient India is perhaps the most accurate and the greatest source for the employed surveyors to measure the Indian Roads. We glean from this source that a road ran from Penkelaotis (Pushkalavati) near the modern Attock passed on through Takshila to Patalipura (Pata) after crossing the river Bias. Another road joined Pushkalavathi and Indra-prastha (Delhi) and after connecting Ujjayini (Ujain) descended down the Vindhya range, went into the Deckan through Pratisthana after crossing the Nerbuda and the Tapty. There were the internal highways of traffic and it was carried on by Uday of the Caravans. Early in India the external and internal commerce had assumed such importance that we find mention in the Buddha Jataka a league of caravan leaders. The caravan leader or Sattravaha in Pali headed the caravan on its journey and was looked to " for directions as to halts, waterning, precautions against robbers, and in many cases as to routes, fords, etc." The journey of the Caravan was mostly by night.

Trade in early India was not entirely individualistic. There is enough evidence to show the corporate commercial activity and partnership in Trade were occasional, if not general. There was very little government control of business and that too only so far as it concerned the Royal purchases. The prices of articles of Royal purchases were fixed by a Royal valuer who would " also assess the merchants for the duty of a twentieth, presumably *ad valorem,* on each consignment of native merchandise, and of a tenth *ad valorem* plus a sample, on each consignment imported from overseas Finally, he would have to assess merchants for their specific commutation of the " rajaksaya " viz. one article per month sold to the king at a certain discount."

Later on however prices came to be fixed: for Manu says that the king on every 5th or 9th day fixed the rates for the purchase and sale of marketable commodities.

The introduction of money in India whether it was borrowed or invented at home is a matter of great controversy : but whatever may be said on this, it is true that the use of money in India was early known for" the whole of the Buddhist literature testifies to the fact that the ancient systems of simple barter as well as of reckoning value of cows, or rice measures had for the most part been replaced by the use of metal currency, carrying well understood and generally accepted exchange value ". Currency counted of coins but was not regulated by Royal authority. There was gold coinage for the most part and " all marketable commodities and services had a value expressible in terms of cash ". Banking was not very highly developed—there was no taboo on loaning of money and according to Gautama interest was sought in six different ways.[f21]

With such high type of economic development it is but natural that there should be commercial expansion of colonization by the Early Hindoos. Historians however have been very reluctant to accept the fact : they have either judging the present by the present rule upon the entire Hindoo population as incapable people or have exerted their utmost ingenuity to discount any evidence that antagonises with their preconceived bias. Isolation of India has been a trump card with them and they use it as often as they can. Environmental conditions do delimit the activity of a people subject to it but it could be foolish to say with Hirder " that history is geography set in motion." We might hold to the truth in the statement that geographic conditions have condemned India to her lot and yet condemn the hyperbole in it.

We may agree, if we like, with Montesquieu when he ascribes the " fixity " of oriental manners, customs and religion to its warm climate. We may believe in Buckle when he holds nature's overpowering mountains and forests in all their stupefying greatness as are to be found in India responsible for the abnormal workings of imagination and superstition or we may follow the scientific geographer when he asserts that India has been condemned to isolation on account of her geographic location : isolated from China by the Himalaya mountains and from Persia and Afghanistan by the Hindu Kush mountains. She has along waterfront but the eastern and the western ghats that fringe the coast from within and cut off the call of the ever beaconing sea to maritime activity.

All these allegations perhaps have a modicum of truth in them: but it would be a mistake to make strong arguments out of them. Barriers, no matter how strong, are never insuperable to man. He has tried everywhere to control them and has succeeded in his effort.

Hemmed in from all sides, the early Indians burst asunder all impediments natural or otherwise and launched into the Indian ocean at a very early date. The Indian ocean has much in common with the mediterranean. Mr. Zimnurn argues that " land locked on all sides ....the mediterranean seems in summer as gentle as an inland lake. .... It is in fact double-natured....... a lake when the Gods are kind, and the ocean when they are spiteful."[f22] The Indian ocean which is but the enlarged mediterranean sea with its southern coast removed is neither a ocean nor a lake but is according to Ratzel only half an ocean. The inclosed character of its northern part deprives it of the hydrospheric and atmospheric peculiarities of a true ocean and the winds and currents ran over it in an unorganised way owing to the close by lands. The North-east and South-east monsoons soon enabled the merchants to drag forth in the mid-ocean instead of hugging to the coast.

"From the dawn of history the northern Indian ocean was a thoroughfare. Alexander the Great's rediscovery of the old sea route to the orient sounds like a modem event in relation to the grey ages behind it Along this thoroughfare Indian colonists, traders and priests carried the elements of Indian civilization to the easternmost Sunda isles; and oriental wares, sciences and religions moved westward to the margin of Europe and Africa. The Indian ocean produced a civilization of its own, with which it coloured a vast semi-circle of land reaching from Java to Abyssinia, and more faintly, owing to the wider divergence of race, the further stretch from Abyssinia to Mozambique."[f23] The Hindus became the dominant commercial nation of the Indian ocean long before the great development of Arabian sea power, and later shared the trade of the East African coast with the merchants of Oman and Yemen. Today they form a considerable mercantile class in the ports of Mascat, Aden, Zanzibar, Pemba and Natal."[f24]

With this preliminary disquisition about the natural resources and the economic development of India we will trace her commercial intercourse from very early times with other countries of ancient civilization.

To begin with Egypt. At the outset it would be better to premise that the evidence of a commercial intercourse between India and other countries at the dim dawn of history is very flimsy and is embedded either in tradition or in articles excavated from early ruins: The evidence however ripens into positiveness with the advance of time.

Situated in the most rarely endowed location in the world the Egyptians were economically independent of the rest of the people—and it is even said that they prided economic self-sufficiency to such an extent that they tabooed foreign intercourse; but this is carrying things too far and though we have no positive records to disprove the statement, the foreign articles found in the process of excavation form a strong proof against it.

It is a matter of great controversy whether or not the Egyptians had direct trade with India. Hypercriticism has ranged on both sides. Herodotus says that Sesostris whom the Gardiner Wilkin-son identifies with Ramses II fleeted out a strong fleet and sailed beyond the straits into the Indian ocean conquering all the coastal countries while his land forces carried their sword as far as the Ganges[f25]

Long before the exodus of the Israelites from Egypt, India had commercial intercourse with her and the port of Philoteras was the emporium of that early trade:

" Whether they (the Egyptians) had a direct communication with India at the same early epoch, or were supplied through Arabia with the merchandise of that country, it is not possible now to determine: but even an indirect trade was capable of opening to them a source of immense of wealth; and that the productions of India did actually reach Egypt we have positive testimony from the tombs of Thebes " [f26] and " the productions of India already came to Egypt at the early period of Joseph's arrival in the country is evident from the spices which the Ishmaclities were carrying to sell there : and the amethysts, hacmatile, lapis'lazuti, and other objects found at Thebes at the time of the Third Thothmus and succeedirig pharaohs argue that the intercourse was constantly kept up."[f27]

Cultwre in all times follows the wake of Commerce. This is more true of ancient times than of the modern. The caravans of the olden times were not only the carriers of wares but also of civilization: they dissiminated and universalized it. This commercial intercourse with India greatly affected the architec-tuie of Egypt so much so that "James Fergusson *(History of Architecture* 7,142-3) notes that thegreatmOttolithatAxurnis ^f Indian inspiration; " the idea Egyptian, but the details Indian. An Indian nine-storied pagoda, translated in Egyptian in the first century of the Christian era! " He notes its likeness to such Indian temples as Bodh-Gaya, and says, it represents" that curious marriage of Indian with Egyptian art which we would expect to find in the spot where the two people came in contact, and enlisted architecture to symbolize their commercial union."[f28]

It will not be out of place to note the relation of the Dravidians, the earliest inhabitants of India though by no means aborigines with the people of western Asia. Mr. GustavOppert says, "It is established now, beyond any doubt, through the decipherment of the Cunciform inscription, that the Turanian Empires had advanced to a high degree of culture. This civilization, though tainted with strange materialism proved itself nevertheless able to develop to a high degree of perfection certain branches of arts and science. To these Turanians who differed much among each other in idiom belong also to the Dravidians of India of our days, who in those times occupied Ariana and Persia. In Europe, these Turanians appear to be represented by the Esthonians, and in many places of western and central Asia, they formed the substratum of the population, while they supplied in China the ground work of the civilization of the celestial empire." These Turanians " had founded empires throughout the old world. The home of the Turanians is assumed to have been the country round Lake Aral. Thence they spread over the greatest part of Asia, reigned there paramount for at least 1500 years." The Egyptians, the Assyrians the Akkadians, the Sumerians, the Phoenicians are all branches of the same Turanian race. " About 250 years after the Egyptian empire had been established i. e. 2500 B. C., and after the Akkadian dynasty had reigned for a long period in Babylon the Aryans invaded Chaldea, and pressing at the same time on the Kannanites of the Persian Gulf and the Dravidians in Persia, drove the former towards the North-west and the latter to the South-east to India ". The Aryans when they invaded India met with a stubborn resistance from these Dravidians. For " they did not go beyond the frontiers of the Punjab till the fifteenth century before Christ "[f29] Next in importance and chronology comes the intetcourse between India the kingdom of India. 'In spite of the evidences to be found in the Bible, writers have been very little disposed to credit it for historical purpose. The evidence is too strong to be slighted "[f30] Suited in the mainland, Judea was not in a position to develop a direct trade with India. She had no water-front at all and consequently no harbours. She had entirely to depend upon the Egyptians and the Syrians who controlled the sea and the trade routes of India. The galleys of India brought their goods to Yemen or Arabia Felix. Yemen was the great mart for Indian goods : it was a distributing centre and from it Indian commodities were taken to Syria by the caravan or to Egypt by the Egyptian Vessels. " From the very earliest ages the refined civilization of Egypt and Syria sought with avidity the spices, the aromatics, the metals, the precious and scented woods, the gems, the ivory in a kind, all the valuable merchandise which the rich soil of India supplied in abundance."[f31] King Solomon, however, when he came to the throne, tried to get the control of Indian trade. He saw that the Egyptian power was on its decline and realized that importance of utilizing Idumeeas sea port on the Red Sea and which had inherited as the conquest of his father— for materialising his plans of direct trade relations with India. But since the Jews had not been experienced in the art of navigation, he had to seek the cooperation of Hirain, the king of the Phoenicians. The Phoenicians were the pioneers in navigation. Whether they dealt directly with India is a subject of great controversy. Mr.Robertsonis favourably inclined. After showing how the poverty of the land compelled the Phoenicians to subsist by commerce, he goes on to say, " among the various branches of their commerce, that with India may be regarded as one of the most considerable and most lucrative as by their situation on the mediterranean, and the imperfect state of navigation, they could not attempt to open a direct communication with India by sea: the enterprising spirit of commerce prompted them to west from the Idumacans some commodious harbours towards the bottom of the Arabian Gulf. From these they held a regular intercourse with India on the one hand, and with the eastern and southern coasts of Africa on the other. The distance, however, from the Arabian Gulf to Zyre, was considerable, and rendered the conveyance of goods to it by land carriages so heavious and extensive that it became necessary for them to take possession of Phinocolura, the nearest port in the mediterranean to the Arabian Gulf, thither all the commodities brought from India were conveyed overland by a route much shorter, and more practicable, than that by which the productions of the East were carried at a subsequent period from the opposite shore of the Arabian Gulf to the Nile. At Rhinocolura they were re-shipped, and transported by an Easy navigation to Tyre, and distributed throughout the world. This, as it is the earliest route of communication with India of which we have any authentic discription, had so many advantages over any ever known, before the modern discovery of a new course of navigation to the east, that the Phoenicians could apply other nations with the productions of India in greater abundance and at a cheaper rate, than any people of antiquity."[f32] Another evidence supporting the view of Mr. Robertson is to be found in the fact, that the Phoenicians introduced their letters in India a direct proof of their intercourse. King Solomon, stimulated or otherwise by the neighbouring Phoenicians, joined hands with Hiram, king of Tyre and built a fleet at Elath and Eziongeher. Manned by Phoenician sailors, it sailed to Qphir and brought backmany treasures which two kings shared between themselves. The location of Qphir is another unsettled topic. But for all practical purposes Prof. Lassen had closed the controversy by identifying it with Abhira in the province of Gujrat in India. With the interval of three years, the voyage was repeated and the ships laden with all precious articles to enrich the country so much so that " the king made silver to be in Jerusalem as stones, and cedars made her to be as Sycamore trees that are in the vale for abundance "[f33] Thus all the advantages of trade were secured for the people with exposing to the dangers attendant upon it. Consequently in the words of Dean Stanley (Senai and Palestine p. 261) "To describe the capital as a place where shall go no galley with oars, neither shall gallant ship pass by " (Isaiah XXXIII 21) is not, as according to western notions it would be, an expression of weakness and danger, but of prosperity and security."

The trade between India and Judea does not date with Soloman: it enjoys considerable antiquity; mentions of Qphir are to be found long before the time of Soloman in the I Chronicles XXIX, 4, I kings XXII 48, and in Isaiah, XIII 12. These Biblical evidences may be supplemented by linguistic evidences, such as the Hebrew word *tuki* which is but a little changed form of the poetical word Tokei i. e. the Tamil-malayalam language for peacock or the Hebrew word *Ahalim* or *Aholoth*—* aloes. *—a corruption of the Tamil-malayalam word, *Aghil*.[f34]

The rise of Babylonia marks the high water mark in the ancient commercial activity of India. Situated at the confluence of the Euphrates and the Tigris joining the Persian Gulf with the mediterranean and being a meeting place of upper and lower Asia, Babylon was destined to be the great emporium of the eastern and western trade. It was the meeting place of routes from all parts of the ancient world. There's ample evidence, says Mr. Kennedy, that" warrants us in the belief that maritime commerce between India and Babylon flourished in the seventh and sixth and more especially in the sixth century B. C. It was chiefly in the hands of the Dravidians, although Aryans also had a share in it, and as Indian traders settled afterwards in Arabia and on the eastern coast of Africa, and as we find them settling at this very time on the coast of China, we cannot doubt that they had their settlements in Babylon also. But the sixth and seventh centuries are the culminating period of Babylonian greatness. Babylon which had been destroyed by Senkacherib and rebuilt by Esarhaddon: Babylon, which had fused her importance and her fame to the sanctity of her temples flow appears before us of a sudden as the greatest commercial mart of the world. There was no limit to her power. She arose and utterly overthrew her ancient rival and oppressor Nineveh. With Nebuchadnezzar she became the wonder of the world......... But the secret of her greatness lay to her monopoly of the treasures of the east, in the shouting of the Chaldeans in their ships and smartly orientals who frequented her lazars. It moved the envy of the nations. * Paharaoh Necho (612-596 B. C.) vainly sacrificed his subjects in order to reopen the canal which Seti I had made from the Nile to the Red Sea : and he despatched his Phoenician fleet round Africa in the hope of discovering a new world for commerce. And a long ago, the rivalry of the Spaniards and the Portuguese for the treasures of India .... was anticipated and equalled by the rivalry of Babylonians and Egyptians.......... when the world was as yet one and twenty centuries younger." [f35] This commercial intercourse told very decidedly on the literature of India. Sea played an immense role and ' *Mokar* ' the monster fish was constantly alluded to. The Vedic dieties fall in the back ground and the Hindu mind of the times soared high in inventing fantastic cosmogonies as is to be found in the Vishnu Purana where it is said that " the Supreme Being placed the Earth on the summit of the ocean, where it floats like a mighty vessel and from its expansive surface does not sink beneath the waters," The entire literature smacks of commercialism and is essentially different in nature from the early Vedic literature so much so that Prof. Max Muller in his *"History of Ancient Sanskrit Literature "* says, " there is throughout the Brahmanas, such a complete misunderstanding of the original intention of the Vedic hymns that we can hardly understand how such an estrangement could have taken place unless there had been at some time or other a sudden and violent breaks in the chain of tradition ". This "estrangement " can be accounted by foreign influence which follows the footsteps of commerce." The focus of this foreign influence upon India was therefore in the sixth, seventh and eighth centuries " and certainly not" later than the time of Buddha, for this great teacher found all India believing in metempsychosis, which is not & Vedic doctrine " and must therefore be an exotic.[f36] It must not however be supposed that the maritime activity of the Hindoos dates from the period : nay sea-farming had become a matter of habit with them : Buddha in the Kevaddhu Sutta of the Digha (fifth century B.C.) says by way of simile" Long ago ocean going merchants were wont to plunge forth upon the sea, on board a ship, taking with them a shore-sighting bird. When the ship was out of sight of land they would set the shore-sighting bird free. And it would go to the east and to the south and to the west and to the north, and to the intermediate points, and rise aloft. If on the horizon it caught sight of land, thither it would go back to the ship again. Just so, brother etc." Mr. Rhys Davids comments that such a Simitic would scarcely be made use of, inordinary talk, unless the habit referred to were of some standing and matter of general knowledge."[f37]

The decline of Babylon however was as sudden as her rise and dates from the reign of king Darius (579-484 B. C.). From the fifth century on, we no longer find the commercial tablets that were so numerous in earlier times. The Persian conquest not only destroyed Babylon but extended to Egypt. The canals build for riverine traffic decayed and the flow of the rivers was impeded by dams : as a result of this the Arabs became the caviers of trade and Yemen interests the splendour of Babylon and Palmyrs   The Chaldeans also in spite of the sweeping expeditions of Darius continued their trade by establishing their colonies at Gerrha and other places.

The conquests Darius brought under his rule a vast Eempire which bacame contiguous with that of the empire of Alexander. It was quite impossible for the two emperors full of earth hunger remain as goodly neighbours, friction was bound to arise and Alexander waiting for an opportunity set out on his career of conquest. In one sweep he destroyed the empire of Darius and extended his dominion over Egypt, Central Asia and the northern part of India.

The motives of Alexander's gigantic expedition are a matter of conjecture. Vindication for humiliation suffered at the hands of Darius has been put forth as one of them. Prof. Lassen, however radically enough, ventures to say that greed of gold was the object of Alexander's expedition and that it was whetted by the presence of Indian goods in Greece. The commercial intercourse with Greece as with Judea has left its impress upon the language of the two trading people." Thus the Greek name for rice (oryza), ginger (zingiber), and cinnamon (karpion) have a close correspondence with their Tamil equivalents, viz., *arisi,* inchiver,and karava respectively; and this identity of Greek with Tamil words clearly indicates that it was Greek merchants who conveyed these articles and their names to Europe from Tamil land. Again, the name *Yavan,* the name by which these Western merchants were known, which in old Sanskrit poetry is invariable used to denote the Greeks, is derived from the Greek word *Jaonis,* the name of the Greeks in their own language." [f38] Another word that may be added to this group of words having a common origin is the parrell words for ivory or elephant in Greek " *Elephas* " in Egyptian " *Ebu* " and " *Ebha* " in Sanskrit which in the opinion of Prof. Lassen indicate a common Sanskrit origin.

Whatever may have been the motives of Alexander, it is quite -certain that having known India intimately, he did conceive the idea of bringing the two countries in close commercial relation. Alexander found that this rich trade of India was monopolized by the Phoenicians of Zyre who supplied the rest of the world with Indian commodities. His envy of the Phoenicians was considerably heightened by his personal knowledge of the prosperity of India. " The country he had hitherto visited, was so populous and well cultivated, or abounded in so many valuable productions of nature and of art, as that part of India through which he had let his army. But when he was informed in every place, and probably with exaggerated description, how much the India was interior to the Ganges, and how far all that he had hitherto beheld was surpassed in the happy regions through which that great river flows, it is not wonderful that his eagerness to view and to take possession of them should have prompted him to assemble his soldiers, and to propose that they should resume their march towards that quarter where wealth, dominion, and fame awaited them." [f39] The northern part of India which Alexander subdued was given over by him to Porus, his ally and is said to have contained " no fewer than four thousand towns." " Even in the most restricted sense" comments Mr. Robertson " that can be given to the vague indefinite appellations of nations and towns, an idea is conveyed of a very great degree of population. As the fleet (of Alexander) sailed down the river (Indus), the country on each side was found to be in no respect inferior to that of which the government was committed to Porus." [f40]

The memoirs or journals of his generals Ptolemy, Aristobulus, and Nearchus opened the knowledge of India to Greece and to Europe. Having conquered Egypt, Alexander thought of opening a direct trade between India and Greece. With this object in view he founded the city of Alexandria after his own name which became the greatest emporium of trade in ancient times and continued to be so in spite of many vissicitudes. He cherished many a dreams of permanently joining

India to his empire and some of it, not all of them, would have been realized had he lived longer. Unfortunately he died soon after he established his empire which within a short time crumbled to pieces. The governors of the different provinces parcelled out among themselves the whole empire. Goaded by ambition, emulation and personal curiosity / animocity they fought among themselves for supremacy. It would be erroneous to suppose that the commercial relation between India and Greece ceased because of the fall of Alexander's empire : just the reverse, the relations became closer. Seleucus, the most enterprising and ambitious general of Alexander, after seizing for himself the Persian empire, sought to join to his dominions the provinces of India conquered by Alexander. Seleucus was alive to the commercial gains to be derived by such a conquest and determined to carry out his plans by means of his vast armies. But his adversary was more than a match for him. Chandragupta (Sandracottus of the Greeks) was ruling India as a benevolent despot. Amidst all medievalism he was a modern man endowed with both brain and brawn. Seleucus realized the superior strength of his enemy and wisely concluded peace and to cultivate friendly relations between the two, he sent Magasthenes as an ambassador to the court of Chundragupta. Magasthenes was followed by Daimachus to continue the friendly relations. The Greeks maintained their intercourse with India through the(Graceo)-Bactrian kingdom for a long time though we have very scanty means to judge its magnitude and charter. The Chinese historians tell us " that about one hundred and twenty-six years before the Christain Era, a powerful horde of Tartars, pushed from their native seats on the confines of China, and obliged to move towards the west by the pressure of a more numerous body that rolled on behind them, passed the Taxartes, and pouring in upon Bactria, like an irresistible torrent, overwhelmed that kingdom, and put an end to the dominion of the Greeks there, after it had been established near one hundred and thirty years "[f41] Though the land communication was thus interrupted, Alexandria continued to be the emporium of sea trade between Greece and India. Ptolemy, the son of Lagus, during his governorship greatly encouraged the Indian Commerce. His son Ptolemy Philadel-phus, in order to carry the articles of India directly to Alexandria started constructing a canal joining the Red Sea and the Nile : the project however was too big and was abandoned. He however built a city on the west coast on the Red Sea and called it Berenice and it continued to be the staple town for Indian trade :

" But while the monarchs of Egypt and Syria laboured with emulation and ardour to secure to their subjects all the advantages of the Indian trade, a power arose in the west which proved fatal to both. The Romans, by the vigour of their military institutions, and the wisdom of their political conduct, having rendered themselves masters of all Italy and Sicily, soon overturned the rival republic of Carthage; A. C. 55, subjected Macedonia and Greece, extended their dominion over Syria, and at last turned their victorious arms against Egypt, the only kingdom remaining of those established by the successor of Alexander the Great."

With the subjugation of Egypt the lucrative commerce from India flowed into Rome; but this was not the only way. There was another trade route for the Indian commodities into the west. It was a land route and was intended by Solomon to concentrate the Indian trade in judea. It passed the town of Tadmore or Dalmyra situated midway between the Euphratis and the mediterranean. After the subjugation of Syria by Romans, Palmyra became independent and grew to be a populous and flourishing town. It became a distributing centre. But the Roman cupidity knew no bounds. At the slightest sign of ill-feeling on the part of Zenobia, the queen of Palmyra, the Romans took the city and ineluded it within their empire.

But the inclusion of Palmyra was not enough for the Romans to monopolize the Indian trade for, another power equally strong was rising into the east. The Parthians had dominated central Asia and had made the boundaries of their empire contiguous with that of the Romans. The struggle between Parthia and Rome extended from 55 to 20 B. C. but the struggle for supremacy remained indecisive. " The warfare between 55 and 20 B. C. had left the two empires with a wholesome respect for each other: and Augustus left it as a principle of imperial policy that the west bank of the Euphrates was the proper limit for the Roman empire, beyond which the power of Rome could not with advantage be extended "[f42] The policy of the Roman Empire during the two centuries following the Christain era was " to encourage direct sea trade with India, cutting out all overland routes through Parthia and thus avoiding the annoyance of fiscal dependence on that consistent enemy of Rome "[f43] Under the Pax Romana, trade between India was greatly fostered and grew so much in importance, guides to the ports of the India and itenerary of land travels and caravans were begun to be written for the benefits of the merchants. It was during the middle of the first century A. D. that Hippolus, a Greek Egyptian, discovered the regularity of the Indian monsoon and thus facilitated the voyage of the traders. It was also about this time that a Greek merchant wrote " The Periplus of the Erythrean Sea " or guide to the Indian ocean. It is the most authentic document we have for the study of the Indian commercial activity. Another Greek adventurer, Isodore of Charax travelled round the Parthian kingdom and gave a full account of the Caravan trade along the land route. Before this it had to receive the oriental goods from the hands of the others. The Arabs concealed all information relating to India to perpetuate their monopoly and the Parthian tolls greatly augmented the" value of the Indian commodities, " so that all this rich trade that flowed to Rome paid its tolls to the empire of Parthia and to the Arab kingdoms, unless Rome could develop and control a sea-borne trade to India "[f44] But this discovery of the monsoons by Hippolus, the columbus of modern times fulfilled much felt want of the Romans." Great shiftings of national power followed this entry of the Roman shipping into the Indian ocean. One by one Petia and Gerrha, Palmyra and Parthia itself, their revenues sapped by the diversion of accustomed trade, fell into Roman hands. The Homerite kingdom in South Arabia fell upon hard times, its capital into ruin, and some to its best men northward and as the Ghassanids bowed the neck to Rome, Abyssinia flourished in proportion as its old enemy declined. If this state of things had continued, the whole course of later events might have changed. Islam might never have appeared, and a greater Rome might have left its system of law and government from the Thames to the Ganges. But the logic of history was too strong. Gradually the treasure that fell to the Roman arms was expended in suppressing insurrections in the conquered provinces in civil wars at home, and in a constant drain of specie to the east in the settlement of adverse trade balances; a drain which was very real and menancing to a nation which made no notable advance in prodtiction or industry by means of which new wealth could be created."[f45]

As regards the Roman trade with India we have a thesaurus of information though by no means unquestionable.

The first kind of evidence is the number of embassies sent to Rome from India and Ceylon.

The first embassy came from Ceylon and is recorded by Pliny. It is impossible to determine its exact date : but certain. circumstantial evidences would warrant us in placing somewhere between A. D. 41 and 54. It was sent to Claudis and reached him at a time when more serious events such as the intrigues of Agrippina and Messalina's violent death too much occupied the minds of the Roman historian to make an adequate mention of it. The embassy was sent by Chundra Muka Siwa King of Celyon who ruled from 44 to 52 A. D.[f46]

Other embassies soon followed. The second came to Trojan in A. D. 107, third to Antonius Pius A. D. 138, fourth to Julian A. D. 361 and the fifth to Justinian A. D. 530. The natives of Indian make no mention of these embassies. They are recorded by Roman historian and barely so, consequently it is very difficult to infer regarding the object of these embassies. They however serve to demonstrate that intercourse between India and Rome was constant and alive and that " during the reign of Servius, his son Commodus, and the pseudoantonines", when Alexandria and Palmyra were both occupied with commerce and were both prosperous. Roman intercourse with India was at its height. Then Roman literature gave more of its attention to Indian matters and did not, as of old, confine itself to quotation from the historians of Alexander or the narratives of the Seleucidian Ambassadors, but drew its information from other and independent sources.[f47]

Other evidences mostly of a literary character strengthen the same conclusion. Dr. Hirth in his "China and the Roman Orient " quotes Sung-Shu, a Chinese historian 500 A. D. writing about the period 420-478 A. D. saying; " As regards Ta-ts'in (Syria) and I'ien Chu (India) far out on the western ocean, we have to say that, although the envoys of the two Han dynasties have experienced the special difficulties of this road. Yet traffic in merchandise has been effected, and the goods have been sent out to the foreign tribes, the force of winds, driving them far away across the waves of the sea. There are lofty ranges of mountains quite different from those we know and a great variety of populous tribes having different names and bearing uncommon designations, they being of a class quite different from our own. All the precious things of land and water come from them, as well as the gems "made of rhinoceros horns and chrysoprase, serpent pearls and asbestos cloth, there being innumerable varieties of these curiosities : and also the doctrine of the abstraction of mind in devotion to the Lord of the world (Buddha)— all this having caused navigation and trade to be extended to these parts."

Another Chinese historian Ma-Touanlin in his Researches into antiquity says "India (A. D. 500-16) carries on a considerable commerce by sea with Ta-Tsin, the Roman empire and the Ansi or ASE". [f48]

A writer of considerable acumen makes bold to say after the destruction of Palmyra, direct trade between India and Rome never existed. The Romans, he says, established their trading station at Adule, the chief port of Ethiopia and " though under Constantine there was much economic prosperity ,yet the Roman trading activity never extended beyond Adule ".

Archaeological discoveries and historical references however point to quite the opposite conclusion. Mr. Vincent Smith remarks; " There is good reason to believe that considerable colonies of Roman subjects engaged in trade were settled in southern India during the first two centuries of our era, and that European soldiers, described as powerful Yavanas, and dumb Mlecchas (barbarians) clad in complete armour, acted as body-guards to Tamil kings, while the large ships of the Yavanas lay off Muziris (Cranganore) to receive the cargoes of pepper paid for by Roman gold "[f49] Not only were there Roman trading colonies but that " Roman soldiers were enlisted in the service of the Pandyas and Other Tamil kings "[f50]. And " during the reign of the Pandya Aryappadai -Kadaretha - Nedunj - Cheliyan, Roman soldiers were employed to guard the jobs of the fort of Madura "[f51] Numismatic evidences also bear out the intimate commercial relations between India and Rome.

(Half page of theM.S.is left blank—
ed.)

This intimate commercial intercourse between Rome and India is very readily accounted for by the fact that " from the time of Mark Antony to the time of Justinian i. e. from B. C. 30 to A. D. 550, their political, importance as allies against the Parthians and Sassanians, and their commercial importance as controllers of one of the main trade routes between the east and the west, made the friendship of the Kusans or Sakas, who held the Indus Valley and Bactria, a matter of highest importance to Rome ".[f52]

With this short sketch of the trade relations of India with foreign countries we will now consider the articles of commerce and trade routes and the important ports of India.

The Periplus, Ptolemy's Geography and the Christian Topography are the chief sources that furnish with information on the articles of commerce and the ports of India.

The Periplus mentions the following as articles of export :

(1) Spikenard, (2) Cortus,(3)Bdellium, (4) Ivory, (5)Qugate, (6) Lycircm, (7) Cotton cloth of all

kinds, (8) Silk cloth, (9) Mallow-cloth, (10) Yarn, (II) Long pepper, (12) Diamonds, (13) Sapphiris, (14) Tortoise shell, (15) Transperent stones of all kinds, (16) Pearls, (17) Malabathrum (18) Incense, (19) Indigo.

Under imports it mentions: (1) Wine,(2) Copper,(3) Tin,(4) Lead, (5) Coral, (6) Thin clothing and Inferior sorts of all kinds, (7) Sweet clover, (8) Flint and crude glass, (9) Antimony, (10) Gold and Silver coins accruing from the favourable balance of trade.

The Periplus or the marine guide book to the Indian ocean mentions the following trading ports of India :

(1) Barygaza or the modem Baroach the principle trading centre of western India. It mentions two inland towns connected with Baroach, Paitlian and Tagara.

(2) Souppara—modern Supara near Bassein.

(3) Kalliean—the present Kalyan.

(4)Semulla—presumably modern Chembur.

(5) Mandagora.
(6) Palaipatami.
(7) Melizeigara.
(8) Tyndis.
(9) Muziris.
(10) Nelkynda.

" Ptolemy's Geography " describes the whole sea coast from the mouths of the Indus to those of the Ganges, and mentions many towns and ports of commercial importance. These are, among others, Syrastra (Surat), Monoglosson (Mangrol) in Guzerat, Ariake (Maharashtra), Soupara, Muziris, Bakarei, Maisoli (Masli-patnam), Kounagara (Konarak), and other places ". [f53]

Certain of the Tamil poets have beautifully described some of the commercial ports and towns in southern India. One of them says, " The thriving town of Muchiri, where the beautiful large ships of the Yavans, bringing gold, come splashing the white foam on the waters of the Periplus which belongs to the Cherala, and return laden with pepper." " Fish is bartered for paddy, which is brought in baskets to the houses," says another. " Sacks of pepper are brought from the houses to the market: the gold received from ships, in exchange for articles sold, is brought to shore in barges at Muchiri, where the music of the Surging sea never ceases, and where Kudduvan (the Chera king) presents to visitors the rare products of the seas and mountains."[f54] The description given of Kaviripaddinam (the Kamara of the Periplus and Khaberis of Ptolemy) or Pukar are equally important and inspiring. It was built on the northern bank of the Kaveri river; then a broad and deep stream in which heavily laden ships entered from the sea without slacking sail. The town was divided into two parts, one of which, Maruvar-Pakkarn, adjoined the sea coast. Near the beach in Maruvar-Pakkarn were raised platforms and godowns and warehouses where the foods landed from ships were stored. Here the goods were stamped with the Tiger stamps (the emblem of the Chola kings) after payment of customs duty, and passed on to merchants ' warehouses. Close by were the settlements of the Yavana (foreign) merchants, where many articles were always exposed for sale. Here were also the headquarters of the foreign traders who had come from beyond the seas and who spoke various tongues. Vendors of fragrant pastes and powders, of flowers and incense, tailors who worked on silk, wool, or cotton, traders in sandal, aghil, coral, pearl, gold, and precious stones, grain merchants, washermen, dealers in fish baits, butchers, blacksmiths, braziers, carpenters, coppersmiths, painters, sculptors, goldsmiths cobblers, and toy-makers all had their habitation in Maravar-Pakkam."[f55]

The trade routes from India to the west may be conveniently divided under two heads. (1) The land routes and (2) The marine route.

It is truly said that individual migration is a habit of civilized man. Ancient folks, because of their strong gregarious instinct or because of the want of security, always moved in bands. This habit of theirs is well depicted in their methods of trade. Compelled to be peddlars, fear of competition was never too strong to break the tradings. Caravan which moved from place to place with their loaded animals under conditions so Unfavourable that easygoing modem man with all the keen business instinct in him will rather quit worshipping the mamon rather than undergo the difficulties ill-compensated by gain. Speaking of the Caravan Mr.Harbursays, " The very course of the Caravan was not a matter of free choice, but of established custom. In the vast steppes'of sandy deserts, which they had to traverse, nature had sparing allotted to the traveller a few scattered places of rest, where, under the shade of palm trees, and beside the cool fountains at their feet, the merchant and the beast of burden might enjoy the refreshment rendered necessary by so much suffering. Such places of repose became centreparts of commerce, and not infrequently the sites of temples and sancturies, under the protection of which the marchants prosecuted his trade, and to which the pilgrim resorted.[f56]Being subject to these conditions the Caravan route was never a straight one, it was always zigzag and when we look at maps of ancient trade we are struck with a network of small roads meeting and crossing each other at various points. However we may decipher two main trade routes from India to the mediterranean. The northern most followed the river Oxus and encircling the northern basin of the Caspian sea converged on the Black sea and thence to Constantinople. The middle one rather followed a straight path, with many bifurcations which meet at market.   It starts on alorig the southern basin of the Caspian Sea through, Tebriz, Erzewm Trebizond and through the Black

Sea to Constantinople. These were the two main land trade routes between the India and the west.

There were also two marine routes though one of them was only halfway marine. Of these one was the Red Sea route. Ships from Indian ports crossed the Indian ocean either to southern Africa or sailed upwards, and touched at the ports of southern Arabia and Aden and through the *St. of Babel-mandeb* (the gate of Tears) ploughed the waters of the Re'3 Sea, touching at Jedda on the Arabian coast and Bernice on the Egyption coast. From Bernice goods were taken by Caravan to Thebes and Kos where they were gained through the Nile to Alexandria and from thence to Europe. The other marine route lay through the Persian gulf. Ships sailed from Baroach and kept bugging close to the land and touched at Masket and at Ormuz through the gulf of Oman to Bassora. From Bassora at the mouth of the Persian gulf, the goods were taken by the Caravan along the shores of the Euphrates and Tygris through Babylonia to Antioch on the mediterranean.

These two marine trade routes continued upto the present tittle but the story of the land trade routes is entirely different. They were closed and were closed for ever and the history of their foreclosure is perhaps the only event in the Asiatic continent that profoundly affected the history of Europe.

[f1]* First page of the MS. is missing. The MS. starts from the 2nd page—ed

[f2]Quoted by Earl of Cromer " Ancient and modem Imperialism ", p. 72.

[f3]* Portion eaten by moth or white-ants is shown by asterisk in brackets—ed. *

[f4]2Ibid.,p.73..

[f5]* Portions in bracket are eaten by termites. Words supplied—ed

[f6] Portions in bracket are eaten by termites. Words supplied—ed

[f7] Portions in bracket are eaten by termites. Words supplied—ed

[f8]W. R. Paterson. " The Nemesis of Nations ", p. 307.

[f9]* Portions in brackets shown by asterisk are eaten by termites

[f10]W. R. Patterson. " The Nemesis of Nations ", p. 334

[f11]' Franz Cumont, Oriental Religions in Roman Paganism, p. 2

[f12]Ibid.,p.6

[f13]*Ibid, p. 8.

[f14]'Ibid.p.9.

[f15]* Portions in brackets shown by asterisk are eaten by termites. Words supplied -ed

[f16]1 Brooks Adams, Law of Civilization and decay, p

[f17]p. 2 R. C. Dutt.

[f18]* Potions in brackets shown by asterisk are eaten by termites. Words supplied—-ed

[f19]• Thompson E. W. "History of India ", p. 2

[f20]* Imperial Gazetteer of India, Vol. 1. p. 215.

[f21]' The information on the early Economic Organisation of India has been borrowed from the article in the Journal of the Royal Asiatic Researches for 1901, p. 859 by Caroline Foley Rhys Davids M. A.

[f22]1 The Great Common Wealth, p. 20.

[f23]' Ellen Churchill Semple—" Influences of Geographic Environment

[f24]", p. 309. 2Ibid.,p.268.

[f25]1 cf. Wailliiam Robertson "Disquisition India ", (1812) p. 6.

[f26]' Gardinaer Wilkinson" The Ancient Egyptions ", Vol. I. p. 161

[f27]* Gardinaer Wilkinson, " The Ancient Egyptions ", Vol. I,,p. 250

[f28]1 " The Periplus of the Erythracan Sea ", Translated and annotated by W. H. Scoff, p. 66-67

[f29]2 of. Gustav oppent, "On the Ancient Commerce of India " in " The Madras Journal of literature and Science "187 8, pp. 189,90,91; for parallels between Malbarian and Egyptian customs of " Primitive Civilizations " by E. J. Sirncox Vol. I, pp. 183. 550,554,569,570. 574, Vol. H, p. 473.

[f30]* of. W. Robertson " Disquisition " p. 9-10

[f31]* I. Lenorment and E. Chevallier, " Ancient History of the East Vol. I,p.144.

[f32]1 W. Robenson " Disquisition " p. 7-8.

[f33]2 I Kings X 27

[f34]* of. E. J. Simcox— "Primitive Civilzations " Vol, I,,p. 545.

[f35]1 J. Kennedy J. R. A. S. 1898, p. 270-1

[f36]. 2 Rev. Joshep Edkins J.R.A.S. 1886. p. 6.

[f37]1J.R. A. S. 1899. Vol. 31, p. 432.

[f38]1 R. K. Mookerji " Indian Shipping " p. 121

[f39]2 W. Robertson " Disquisition ". p. 16-17.

[f40]1 W. Robertson " Disquisition " p. 22

[f41]1 W. Robertson "Disquisition " p. 37

[f42]1 Isidore of Charax " Parthian Stations " ed. W. H. Schoff, p. 21.

[f43]2Ibid,p. 19

[f44]1 Periplus of the Erythrean Sea, W. H. Schoff, p. 5

[f45]2 Erased

[f46]1 of. J. R.A. S. 1860 Vol. XVIII, p. 349-50.

[f47]2 of J. R. A. S. Vol. XIX. p. 276

[f48]1 Quote in the J. R. A. S. Vol. XIX, p. 307

[f49]2 Early History of India, p. 400-1

[f50]Quoted in Mookerjee's Indian Shipping, p. 128.

[f51]1 Quoted Ibid. p. 128.

[f52]2 Quoted in Mukerjee—" Indian Shpping ", p. 139.

[f53]1 R. K. Mookerjee "Indian Shipping ", p. 134

[f54]2 Quoted in Ibid, p. 135

[f55]1 Mookerjee R. K. " Indian Shipping ", p. 135-136

[f56]2 Quoted in the Calcutta Review , Vol 19, p. 345 .